abide
CLARITY IN THE LONGING

For the Lord gives wisdom;
from his mouth come knowledge and understanding;
he stores up sound wisdom for the upright;
he is a shield to those who walk in integrity,
guarding the paths of justice
and watching over the way of his saints.

- Proverbs 2:6-8

Copyright © 2021 Shannon Guerra

With gratitude to the contributing authors, who each retain the copyright for their individual works.

All rights reserved. No part of this book may be reproduced in any form or by any electronic or mechanical means, including information storage and retrieval systems, without permission in writing from the publisher, except by reviewers, who may quote brief passages in a review.

ISBN 978-1-7360844-4-1 (paperback)
      978-1-7360844-5-8 (ebook)

Published by Copperlight Wood
P.O. Box 870697
Wasilla, AK
99687
www.copperlightwood.com

Design by Shannon Guerra. Photography by Shannon Guerra, with the exception of page 25 by Cynthia Hellman and pages 59-60 by Megan Ancheta.

Unless noted otherwise, scripture quotations are from the ESV® Bible (The Holy Bible, English Standard Version®), copyright © 2001 by Crossway, a publishing ministry of Good News Publishers. Used by permission. All rights reserved.

Portions of scripture in **bold** are the author's emphasis.

This title may be purchased in bulk for ministry or group study use. For more information, please email shop@copperlightwood.com.

Printed and bound in the USA.

contributors

MĒGAN ANCHETA
Kodiak kid, owner of two exuberant labs and Allergy Free Alaska, LLC
www.allergyfreealaska.com
allergyfreealaska@gmail.com

ROBIN ANGAIAK
happy human, wild Alaskan salmon snob, spreadsheet magician
www.lineandledger.com

JESSICA DASSOW
wrangler of many boys and a princess, chicken collector, seeker of sand & sunshine
www.planted-by-the-river.com

CYNTHIA HELLMAN
laundry avoider, alpaca owner, timid adventure seeker
www.cultivatedgraftings.blogspot.com

RENEE PETTY
barefoot hiker, bee tamer, tiller of soil, dances in the kitchen and laughs at her own jokes

contents

06
toward victory

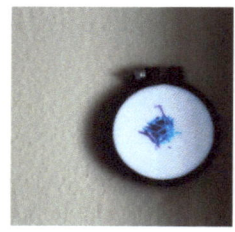

10
one stitch at a time

14
He makes us to see

17
sounding it out

22
it's okay to be quiet

24
a surrendered focus

27
out of the comfort zone, into the mess

31
on dreams and desires

32 murky waters   **36** seeing what isn't there   **42** be Thou my vision   **44** bedrock: when nothing is working

50 at His word   **53** doing the work   **56** favorite salad & croutons   **59** vegan, gluten free banana bread

61 the fruit we bear   **66** colossians 1:9-10   **68** study guide   **75** notes

toward victory

It was the second time I'd ripped out this knitting project, which meant it was going to be the third time I started over from scratch. But it had to happen because every row felt less and less beautiful, farther away from what it should be.

So I spent forty minutes unraveling yarn, ripping out weeks of work. I regrouped colors. Got a new vision. Changed the pattern. And when I started over this time, I did so with hope, joy, and renewed purpose – even though the end result was going to look entirely different from what I originally planned…like so many things in life.

But I kept working at that knitting in progress, and when it was time to change colors, I was right here in my Bible reading:

> *Aspire to live quietly, and to mind your own affairs, and to work with your hands, as we instructed you.*
> — 1 Thessalonians 4:11

If you don't know, knitting tends to be slow work. Especially garter stitch, especially the same color row after row. But it produces something — just like pages read, prayers prayed, and Scripture spoken.

They all *do* something. They produce results. They create and refine things (and us). But sometimes it takes a while to see that progress. Which is all the more reason to start today.

So we pray. We read books. We speak Scripture. We move in faithful obedience.

How good of Him to not just create light, but to also give us color. We make all these little stitches, and we know that it makes the Kingdom come in a powerful way. Pretty soon, we'll see the colors start to change. We'll see the conversations start to make an impact. We'll see the Scripture start to sink in, and then bubble up out of us when we need to recall it.

When we start a project — whether it's knitting, or writing, or building, or painting, or teaching, or any other creative endeavor — we are working toward something we cannot see. We aren't disgusted or despairing that the blanket isn't complete yet after a few rows of stitches, because we know it's a process. We see the unseen, and we work toward it.

And this is how prayer works, too.

> *A hundred times a day our thoughts turn Godward in penitence, in desire, in fear, in aspiration, and – this is a truly delightful thought – in sympathy. Our hearts glow with delight at the blue of a gentian, the glory of a star, the grace of some goodness that we get news of: we lift up our hearts to the Lord, though without a word; and the throb is one of sympathy, for we know that His delight, also, is in beauty and goodness.*
> — Charlotte Mason[1]

If you are praying for some big thing — or struggling with something major, or discouraged over huge current events — remember, we partner with God to work toward things that are unseen, and they change.

We pray from victory, and we pray toward victory. And it works.

But do you ever feel so overwhelmed with the desperate need to pray for all the things that it keeps you from praying at all? We have no idea where to start. There's so much to pray for. How much can we really do? And we feel so behind in praying, anyway.

Let me tell you something: Those are not your thoughts. Those are lies from the enemy intended to keep you from praying because the enemy is terrified of what happens when you pray.

Things change when you pray. Physically, spiritually, emotionally, things shift and align with God's good will when we pray.

So just start right now. Just pray the first thing that comes to mind. And then the next.

And then the next.

Right as you're reading, as you're turning pages, as you feel breath move in and out of your body, just say something to Him. And listen for His response. Every prayer, every minute matters.

Be quick to run back to the Lord. He's not angry with you for starting over, for getting distracted, for falling asleep, or for tending to your children or other work. He is so near, ready to give us His thoughts – because we have the mind of Christ[2]– so we can agree and partner with Him in the great, effective, powerful work of prayer. He will show us what we're creating with Him soon enough.

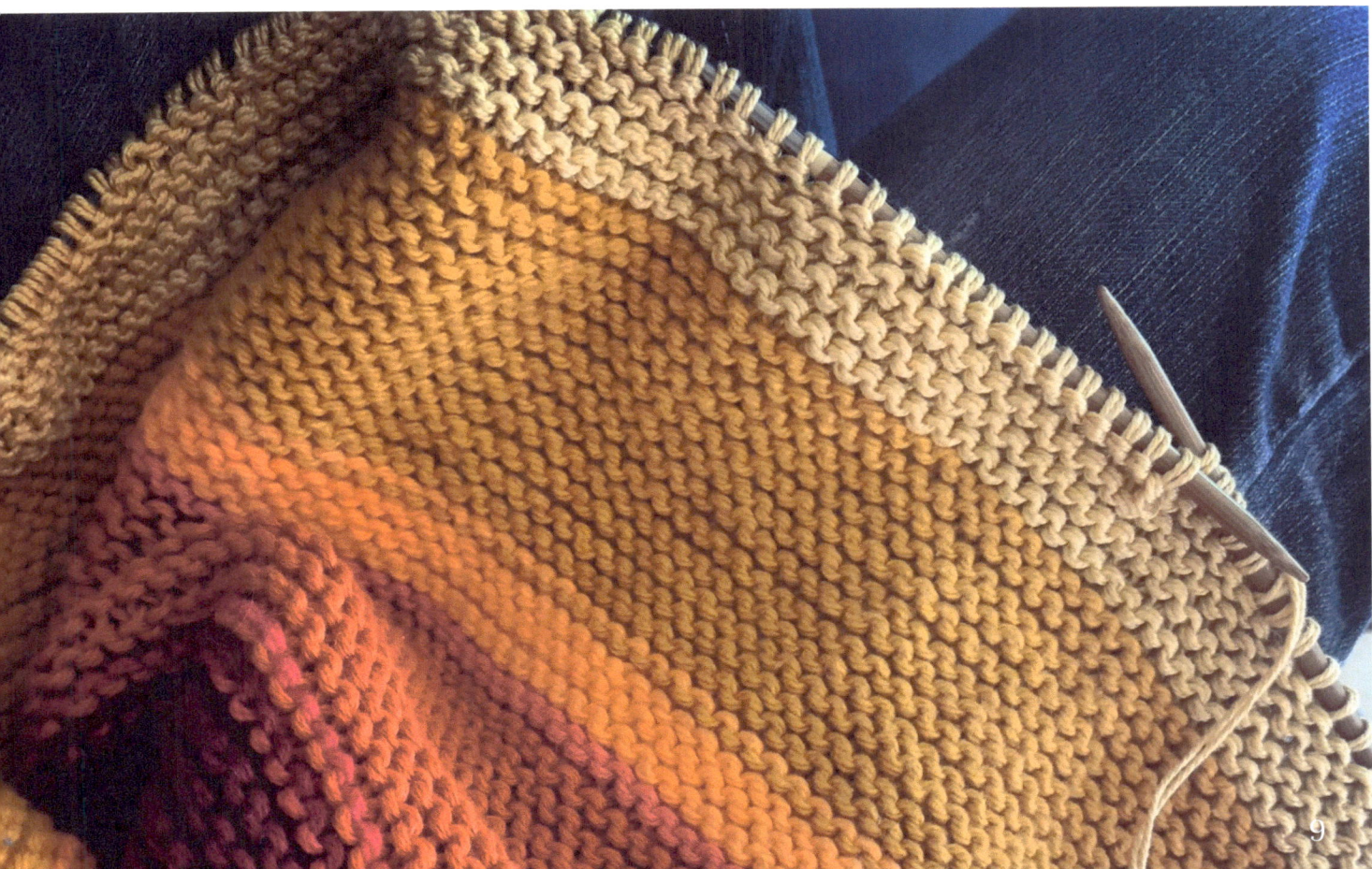

one stitch at a time

To comma or not to comma, that is the question.

After I homeschool the kids in the morning, my workday is only a few hours long and I spend much of it choosing between periods and semicolons, fixing dashes, and trying to decide where commas go. I stare at sentences and pray for the right words. And I delete almost as much as I type.

It doesn't feel super significant, or ambitious, or influential. It doesn't even feel like writing. (It is, though. Trust me. If anyone gives you a glamorous, free-and-easy vision of writing, they're either lying, inexperienced, selling something, or a combination of all three.)

But the significant moves in our lives don't usually come with a flashing milepost. I talk and write often about the satisfaction of stitchery because it is a terrific depiction of the slow, steady moves of obedience in our lives.

With something tangible and concrete, you can see how much is actually done. DONE. It doesn't matter if the project still has miles to go; you can clearly see what's already finished. And when so much in our lives is never truly done – like writing, editing, chores, teaching, ministering, or disciplining kids – it's wonderful to have one achievement that's clear cut.

It's the tedious little parts of life that make up the big parts. Our great moves are accomplished just one stitch at a time. Just one word at a time. Just one conversation, one consequence, one load of laundry at a time.

You and I are doing big, significant things with our daily, small, steadfast moves of obedience. So keep going.

We are significant, powerful, and important because He made us that way. We don't always act in alignment with that identity, because of other external issues...but we can, when we remember what our identity really is.

Your identity — who you are — is who He made you. It's who we are, not what we do. What we do is important, but it flows out of who we already are, not the other way around.

Our identities don't change based on our circumstances, our failures, or the failures of others. Our identities don't depend on our feelings or moods.

Our identity doesn't change based on how people treat us, or what others say about us. It's not changed by who we know, or who we don't know. The people we hang out with *do* change us – so go deep with good ones – but our identity is secure regardless of our circle, because He is our circle.

I have to remember this on days when I fight my own limitations, or the limitations of others. On any given day, I might have a kid who tests the limits of my sanity, so I'll keep my grits from getting cooked by focusing on other things: The other kid carving a whistle, another kid reading *To Kill a Mockingbird*, the lazy kitten stretched across the couch napping, the young adult building his resume, the pretty rounds of color taking shape on a new blanket. Some days that's just all you can do, and on those days, it has to be enough – because He is enough, and He has made us enough.

My identity isn't less-than because of what my kids or I accomplish. And this is good news, because if He has called me to do things I can't do on my own, that means He will arrange the doing.

We are in Him, and He is in us, and we are

loved
chosen
valued
purposeful
fought for
redeemed
and equipped with
every spiritual blessing
in His great inheritance.

All those feelings that derail us are important and need to be acknowledged, but they're not the boss of us. They don't change reality.

> *Praise be to the God and Father of our Lord Jesus Christ,* who has blessed us in the heavenly realms with every spiritual blessing in Christ. For he chose us in him before the creation of the world to be holy and blameless in his sight. In love he predestined us for adoption to sonship through Jesus Christ, *in accordance with his pleasure and will— to the praise of his glorious grace, which he has freely given us in the One he loves.*
> — Ephesians 1:3-6

God knows what He's gotten us into. When we ask Him and give Him time, He sorts out the colors and untangles all our threads, and sometimes He does it faster than we could imagine. He knows all of our limits – the real ones, and the ones we impose on ourselves. We've been made with structure, with a framework that hems us in both for our protection and for our growth. Think of a trellis for pea vines: That trellis sets a limit on the direction the vines can grow. But without that structure, the vines will wander all over the ground to wander, to be trampled, to be further from the sunlight they need to grow.

And if you feel stuck and don't know where to go, ask God for His vision for you. Confess to a trustworthy, humble friend, and ask them to pray for you. Then just do the next thing in front of you. These small steps of faithfulness are what prepare us for big steps later.

He makes us to see
BY JESSICA DASSOW

"You've missed your window of opportunity. He's past the age where we can expect to see any positive change. You needed to see us sooner; the counsel you've received and the route you've taken thus far for 'treatment' just wasn't the best way to treat this condition."

I left the ophthalmologist's office fighting tears, trying not to let my son see the struggle and hopelessness I felt. I felt like a bad mom, thinking over the prior six years' worth of running several times per week to vision therapy, occupational therapy, and eye doctor appointments in three different states. I had done home therapy and exercises of all sorts for years. Kept track of all sorts of nutritional supplements. Changed out eyeglass prescriptions multiple times per year, not to mention navigating those interesting times of trying to keep glasses on my 2-year-old's face. It had been so hard.

And it wasn't enough. It wasn't even, according to this specialist, right at all. And now we were too late. I felt crushed, longing to see all this effort lead to some sort of happy ending for my son. Wanting to see that it had all been worthwhile.

I slid into the van, put some music on for my son, and let the tears fall…gush, really…you know, the ugly kind. I texted the news to a couple people I knew were waiting and praying. And I prayed for help.

I heard that kind, quiet voice in my heart ask, "Who told you that? Who told you that it's too late? That you're a bad mom?"

Jolted into reality and feeling a bit shocked at hearing those questions when I really just wanted a heavy dose of comfort – or to be honest, pity – I tried to figure out who, in fact, it was that "told me that." The obvious answer was the specialist whose office I just left…but something inside me knew that while the words came from her voice, the condemnation came from something deeper than human words. The condemnation hissed from the enemy of my soul, having seen a point of entry to my thoughts in my fear and disappointment.

I repented of believing the accusation and lies, and then I looked to my Father for His words concerning the matter. The truth is, it is never too late.

> *And we know that for those who love God all things work together for good, for those who are called according to his purpose.*
> *– Romans 8:28*

Throughout the next days, weeks, and months, we carried on, prayerfully considering our next steps – nutritional testing, different supplements, eye patch therapy, another specialist's opinion, and a slightly different Occupational Therapy plan. All of these things came about one at a time, through a prayerful moment, or something I came across in my reading, or a name dropped by a friend. We couldn't see what the outcome would be, but the clarity of each new step was enough. One step of faith at a time, leaving the outcome to Him.

The experts had said we were too late. Our son was too old. We'd wasted our time with alternative treatments. But ours is the Great Physician. He decides.

Recently, I took my son for a recheck with our new ophthalmologist. My son's vision, which had been 20/100 with correction, is now 20/40 with correction! We'll keep the course, and perhaps there will be even greater improvement.

It's the happy outcome we've been hoping and praying nearly eight years for. We're grateful and our faith is strengthened in His kindness and provision, but even had the outcome been different and our longing left unmet, one thing would still be crystal clear – we need to listen to His voice only. You see, it's so easy to find ourselves listening to the wrong voices – of condemnation and lies – even when we don't mean to or want to. Something shakes our confidence, a little fear creeps in, and suddenly we're thinking nonsense like "I'm a bad mom" or "I've messed this up beyond repair."

"Who told you that?" It's a good question to ask ourselves, especially in emotional moments when our minds are spinning, the tears are falling, and we can't see the way forward. Then listen for that still, small voice…that quiet one, laden with peace, and speaking to your soul. It's that voice that clears our minds and sharpens our focus. It figuratively, and sometimes even literally, makes us to see.

sounding it out

It took us fifteen months of working together from home until we finally discovered a routine that worked. Granted, those months included being pregnant and having a baby and taking on a small ministry and dealing with everything else in life, but still, it seemed like a ridiculously long time to figure it out. I'm actually hesitant to tell you what we discovered because it's so simple, it's stupid. But it made all the difference:

Vince works mornings, I work afternoons.

That's it. Stupid simple, I told you.

Why did it take us so long to hit this stride? Partly because we were afraid to make the change. It was easier (or, it *seemed* easier, which is an entirely different thing) to spread the day thin and just work whenever we could and do whatever needed to be done with whatever time we had. It was both of us at the same time, taking turns helping kids with school, reading stories to the littles, holding and burping the baby, grabbing whatever computer time we could.

It wasn't completely ineffective. I mean, over the first eight months, we published four books and had a baby. Not too bad.

But it felt like striving. It felt like competing for time to work. It felt like constantly neglecting parenting, housework, homeschool, ministry, or writing at the expense of doing any one of those same things. It felt like being a slave to opportunity cost.

And we knew we were missing something, but we couldn't put our finger on it.

It was the old trick I learned as a kid at summer camp. Our leaders gave us this slow chant to repeat: *Owa...tagoo...siam*...and then they told us to say it a little faster, and then a little faster...and after saying it over and over, we finally realized what we were saying. *Oh, what a goose I am.*

The same thing happened when our son encountered the written word "popsicle" – a word he knows but had never read before. He put all the sounds together but could not hear the word he was saying until I took a video of him reading it aloud and then played it back for him. Then the lightbulb went off.

The following week it was our daughter, crying and stressing out over trying to read "UP" – an easy word, a word she knows, a word we use all the time. But she has special needs, and sounding it out while also putting all the pieces together is hard for her.

"What does it say? Just say the sounds," I told her.

"U...p? Up?" She looked at me with raised eyebrows.

"Up! Yes! What is *up*?"

"A movie?" she said, eyebrows still raised. Ah, of course. *This is all your fault, Pixar.*

We see the letters and say the sounds, and we might even be saying them correctly but it takes a while for our ears to recognize the words. *Ahhh, yes, there it is. I had it all along.*

Once we figured out our stupid easy schedule, I could do more in four hours than I had been able to accomplish in two days. And I had more peace and joy in doing it, instead of feeling like I was constantly stealing time and attention from something (or someone) else.

Now faith is the assurance of things hoped for, the conviction of things not seen.

And without faith it is impossible to please him, for whoever would draw near to God must believe that he exists and that he rewards those who seek him.

– Hebrews 11:1 & 6

I'm sure it's no coincidence that I started reading Hebrews again in that season. When I got to chapter eleven, which I've read dozens of times, I saw it with new eyes.

By faith Noah, being warned by God concerning events as yet unseen, in reverent fear constructed an ark for the saving of his household.

By faith Abraham obeyed when he was called to go out to a place that he was to receive as an inheritance. And he went out, not knowing where he was going.

– Hebrews 11:7a & 8

They obeyed, not seeing. Not knowing what the end was going to look like or where they were going to end up. Not understanding how certain things were possible. But they sounded out their steps of obedience, just like we do every time He calls us to something new.

And it's hard. Fighting anxiety in the wee hours, I've wrestled all night with perfect love casts out fear $_3$ – if we have perfect love, we aren't afraid of anything. But to be honest, I struggle with fear when I can't see where we're going. I am afraid of missing His direction, or of confusing His direction with what I want, anyway.

I've noticed that as He calls our family to new things, I go round and round with Him, struggling to put into words what I really want – because I want His desires for me, but I still struggle with trusting myself to know His desires and separate them from my own. And that, too, feels like striving.

But if we are asking God to make our desires the same as His, shouldn't we expect them to come into alignment? Why do we treat such alignment with suspicion?

I want things to turn out a certain way. And sometimes that's the way He wants it to turn out, too, but sometimes it isn't, and things end up in a way I didn't expect. And that is also okay, because I am still learning to sound out His words.

A year earlier, our baby was in utero. So tiny and unseen, unknown – and now he is both seen and known, growing, laughing, moving. The evidence and reward of things hoped for.

When we couldn't see where we're going, He said, *Hold on, Love. Just wait. I told you I've got this – you have no idea how well I've got this. Get ready, you're gonna love this.*

We don't have to fear missing His direction, because perfect love means understanding that He is big enough to make His direction heard in our lives as we abide with Him. When the time is right, we'll be able to put our finger on it. And sometimes it will suddenly seem so obvious, we'll think, *Oh, what a goose I am. I had it all along.*

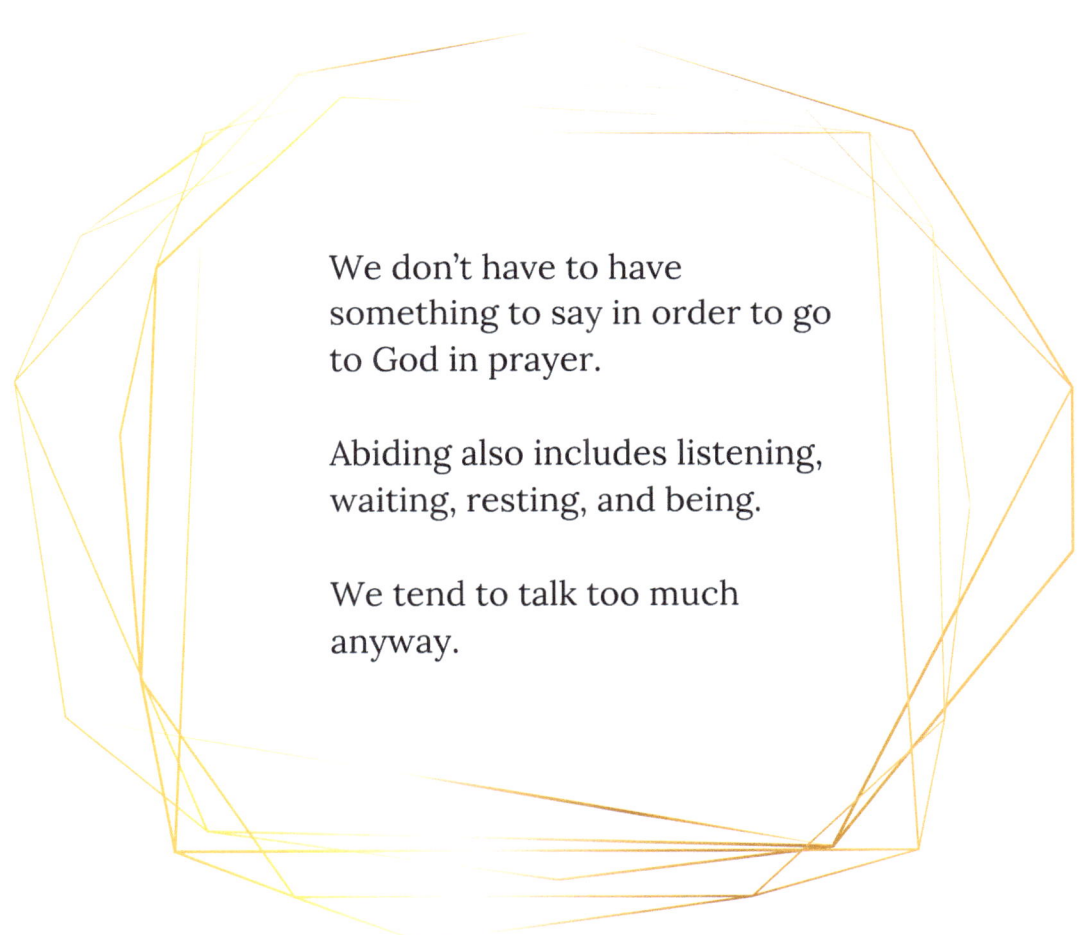

We don't have to have something to say in order to go to God in prayer.

Abiding also includes listening, waiting, resting, and being.

We tend to talk too much anyway.

a surrendered focus

BY CYNTHIA HELLMAN

I fancy myself an amateur birdwatcher.

When my family lived in a concrete maze of city blocks, our exposure to avian variety was… underwhelming. Moving to an outlying area provided us with greater diversity than the typical common pigeon. (Pro tip: If you want to horrify/impress someone, refer to boring ol' pigeons as "rock doves.") We upped our game when we moved to dirt roads and open land. I purchased a bird identification book for our region. Like a good little homeschooler, I strategically placed it on the coffee table, and for months we would spot a new bird, run to the book, run back to the bird and furiously thumb through the pages, racing against the erratic whims of a creature whose brain is the size of its eyeball. More often than not, the thing would take flight before we'd settled on a positive ID. I would click my tongue as we returned to humdrum chores or assignments. *We'll look it up on the internet after school.*

Unidentified winged creature: 1. Me: 0.

Our enthusiasm waned until one day a friend asked if we would be interested in a pair of binoculars. What a delightful invention binoculars are! Yes please, and pass the bird book. We were back in business. (Confession: We've spied on the entire neighborhood just as much as we've identified the local wildlife.) Since becoming the proud owners of a pair of vintage binoculars, we've enjoyed the beauty of God's winged creation…even when they take flight mid-identification.

Ironically, some of our most enjoyable encounters with birds haven't been experienced through the lens of any contraption. We have a pair of roadrunners who, well, *run* around our property. We've observed their behaviors, personalities, and (rather disturbing) eating habits up close and personal. Roadrunners have been known to take down rattlesnakes, so we thank them, supply them with Acme catalogs, and admire the creativity of our God.

Thanks to the generosity of our friends, we've lessened the gap between the magnificence of the moon's surface and our own two feet here on earth. We've chuckled at the silly antics of ground squirrels and bunnies, watched baby quail scurry after their mamas and papas, and wondered why we couldn't see anything when we left the lens caps on. Been there, done that.

We've had to teach our daughters the fine art of adjusting their focus — and not just on binoculars. All too often we hear a frustrated sigh followed by, "I can't see anything. It's not there anymore!" *I assure you, child, the bird I can see with my naked eye is still perched on the same branch he was on when I handed the binoculars to you.* I stand behind her, gently align her vision, and adjust her focus. Sometimes she resists moving, not trusting my guidance. Sometimes she's positive I'm not helping.

And that's when God whispers to me. *You see, my daughter, but you do not comprehend.*

Just like you, I have longings carried deep in my soul, things I whisper to God and wonder what He thinks of it. I have longings I *know* He wants fulfilled — loved ones He desires to gather under His banner of saints. I have longings, faded from hanging them out to air for years on end. I also have fresh, new longings still vibrant with spunky hope bubbling up to join the array. Sometimes the cacophony of longings sends me whirling in all directions, eyes darting while seeing nothing. *God, I can't see Your hand!*

I know He's just standing there, arms akimbo, a fatherly smile of wisdom on His face, waiting to see me surrender my own efforts. When I relinquish control, when I become clay in the Potter's hands, He can gently reorient my position. And (after removing the lens cap for me) He realigns my vision to His. He puts His truth before my eyes and it comes into startling clarity after my own paltry attempts.

Dear friends, He knows what you're longing for. The deepest clarity is found in the greatest surrender to the King of Kings. In El Roi — the God who sees you and knows you intimately. Consider this your invitation, your permission, your exhortation to loosen your hold on that longing. In so doing, you may discover a refined focus, a sanctified vision, and an unshakeable peace.

out of the comfort zone, into the mess

The conversation always starts the same way:

"What do you do for a living?"

"Oh, I'm a writer."

"Wow, what do you write?"

Usually at this point I fumble with an awkward answer involving books, newsletters, and snarky posts on social media. But several times I've been tempted to finish it like this:

"Actually, nothing. I get a few hundred words in, and then my computer is highjacked with random updates for the next three hours while I ponder a future of providing for my family by selling giant homemade peanut butter cups on the black market." Because we all want to live the dream, but few things go as we expect them to. And it turns out, the dream is a ton of work.

Over the last decade our family went through several life-changing, sometimes devastating transitions. We learned how to live in isolation. We learned to live with the unexpected. We learned how to deal with extreme limitations. We learned how to live without supports that many other families have.

And in the more recent years of owning a business and writing full time, we've learned to live with unpredictable (read: sometimes nonexistent) income. We've learned how to make routines that work for both of us — and eight kids — as we've navigated the difficult dream of doing work and ministry together at home.

Easy?

No way. Not for a single minute.

But it's been so good. I'm learning again that we can trust Him. We can do new, brave things we never would've considered before.

On a good week, we start by clearing the rubble out of the way: Repenting, searching, asking God about those stuck places and what needs to be removed for Him to flow through again. I feel so inept at this, but He meets us when we recognize our weakness rather than when we pretend expertise.

Friends, every dream has come with more work than I could have imagined, and it takes more dedication than I sometimes think I have. I've learned to hold my expectations with an open hand, because without surrendering the dream to God, it becomes an idol – and then a nightmare. If we ask Him to use us, we must also allow Him to move us in ways we could not have expected.

But even still, God wants us to dream. He doesn't put these things inside us to tease us. If you find yourself up late at night, thinking of new ideas and new dreams that He's giving you, and you have no idea what to do with them, write them down and look them straight in the face. You can put them on screen or on paper, but at least give them some tangible words.

> *And the Lord answered me: "Write the vision; make it plain on tablets, so he may run who reads it.*
> *- Habakkuk 2:2*

Ask Him if it's for real, if it's for now, if it's for just you, or if it's for you and some others He's also talking to. Tell Him He can do what He wants with it. Get gutsy, go all out, and tell Him He can throw you right outside the small margin of comfort zone you might have recently recovered, and pitch you right into His exciting, marvelous, bigger-than-we-could-possibly-come-up-with-on-our-own mission.

But friends, that dream you long for? That calling you're working toward? That victory you've prayed for? You have to choose between it and the comfort zone, because they do not mingle, they take each other's oxygen, and only one of them finds victory in surrender.

He is always growing us as far as we are willing to move.

Just because things don't look the way you expected doesn't mean you failed. It means you're not perfect at predicting the future (which you're not meant to be) or controlling outcomes (which you're not meant to do).

If you are struggling with these transitions, please know that it takes time to settle into routines that work. It takes trial and error, and the error doesn't mean failure. It means growth. It means you're getting closer to the solution that puts all the pieces in the right place.

For those of us waiting for a labor to end, and for the promise of fullness to come to fruition: There is a messy beauty to works in progress. And we are all a work in progress.

This season is teaching you to let go of those expectations and trust God. It doesn't mean you lower your standards; it means you raise your eyes. You are learning to look past this present circumstance to see His vision for you...which is bigger than you imagined.

Man dreams and desires;
God broods and wills and quickens.

When a man dreams his own dream,
he is the sport of his dream;

When Another gives it to him,
that Other is able to fulfill it.

– George MacDonald [4]

murky waters

BY ROBIN ANGAIAK

We were clear about one thing, we had to go.

We had never rafted. We had rarely camped with our six kids. We were given no detailed plan, except to show up and share our story. We knew enough about Jesus' faithfulness that He could be trusted and would provide everything we needed when we needed it. But we had to step out if we wanted to experience it.

So, a few years ago, our family of eight rafted six hundred miles of the Yukon River, stopping in villages to share what God has done in our family. My husband is Yu'pik and felt called to share with other Native Alaskans what we have experienced as a family – in short, a radical transformation from brokenness to wholeness, not only my husband and I, but kids included.

The brilliance of this plan solved problems like transportation costs, food and lodging issues, and getting an invitation into these villages. A family floating into town on an open raft is welcome; we rowed our rafts and only had to take one flight home, so the travel cost was minimal, and we carried our food and tents. For seventy days we floated and rowed down the Yukon River and met so many amazing people. It *sounds* dreamy and for sure it was beautiful, inspiring and delightful.

But...reality. While I know God delighted in our family's obedience, He's such an opportunist and He used everything about this adventure to expose and deal with our doubts, unbelief and fears.

At one point our launch was delayed for two weeks because of a family emergency. It didn't even phase me and my response was far more in keeping with Jesus than my flesh. I was grateful and thankful! And then, twelve hours before we were to head out and launch, another family emergency ensued and we were further delayed to the tune of four. more. weeks. Twenty-eight days.

Alaskan summers are short. We missed our opportunity to learn how to raft – or at the very least, test the rafts out in a river. People had donated large amounts of money for this trip to happen. We had closed down our business and quit our jobs. We only had food that was made for cooking over a fire.

The second delay brought me to a place of desperation. Nothing was clear. Not staying. Not going. Nothing. In fact, maybe we had heard wrong in the first place.

From the beginning, for almost ten months, the only thing the Lord would tell me was, "Trust Me."

When the first delay hit, I went to Him asking for a word to hang onto. He said, "Trust Me, more." When the second delay happened, He said, "Trust Me, even more." Whaaat? I had nothing else to trust with. There was no plan B here. No backup or alternate route. There was only go or no go.

I heard a teaching on the radio during this time and it was about how God never wastes a word.

And I thought, Well, He is giving me four words, what could I be missing?

That night I looked up the word "trust," specifically the Hebrew word used in Proverbs 3:5: "*Trust* in the Lord with all your heart and don't lean on your own understanding..." *That* trust. *Batah*. Further down the page in the lexicon, it referenced "being thrown on one's back." [5] A vulnerable and exposed position.

Although I had no plan B, I wasn't quite at the "throwing myself down" stage...until that moment. While the mission didn't feel clear, *surrender* was crystal clear.

In the throes of longing and yearning, I keep finding clarity in the nature of Jesus, in who *He is* and who that makes me. I made a choice in that moment to not get hung up on operational details, but instead to get completely tangled up in surrender and trust and faith.

We still don't have a plan B, the details are still fuzzy, but *I know whom I have believed and am persuaded that He is able.*[6] Always. Everyday.

seeing what isn't there

One of my favorite games is a wooden, tactile version of Sudoku that uses colored balls instead of numbers. My oldest daughter and I are fairly addicted, and on a quiet afternoon you'll find one or both of us on the couch trying to master the universe through defeating this puzzle. Once, I solved level 88 all by myself in less than an hour. But don't get too impressed, because that same day I put one of my socks on upside down (you know, heel up), lost my water glass 231 times, and tried to open the post office box with our house key.

Our Sudoku board has over a hundred puzzles to solve that get increasingly difficult the higher you go. If you're not familiar with it, the game is pretty straight forward: In a 9x9 grid, each number (or in this case, color) can only appear once in each row, column, and 3x3 square. In the easy levels you solve this by a simple process of elimination based on the numbers and colors already in place, and the progression of answers is fairly obvious. *If light green can't be here or here, then it must go here.*

The important thing to remember is that you absolutely cannot afford to make a move based on guessing; you have to be certain. Otherwise you'll make a mess of things and have to start over.

But what about when it's not obvious? What about when there's not nearly enough information to go on? What about when life is too confusing – oh, wait, we're talking about Sudoku – and you don't see any options?

I can't tell you how many times I've felt like the solution to a dilemma was just out of reach, like a riddle whose answer is on the tip of my tongue. If I could just figure out how to rearrange things properly or notice the right detail, the "aha" moment would arrive and everything would fall into place.

But I *can* tell you it happens at least once a year, because I've noticed a pattern in my life. Every time I finish a big project after months of hard running, I suddenly have room to rest, which should be a good thing – it *is* a good thing. But instead, I feel aimless, unsettled, and floppy without anything due.

Because I do not know what my next move is.

The last time this happened, on the first day of my quasi-freedom, I puttered all afternoon: a little filing here, some graphic design there. A little walking, a little rearranging things. I wondered about new ideas and asked God for strategy.

And He told me that this wonder and restlessness also counts as abiding, because it, too, is seeking Him – especially when the fog closes in again and we're not sure which direction to take. It puts us back in the waiting, which is some of the hardest abiding we can do. We don't want to move for the sake of moving because we know how dangerous a wrong turn can be, but we can't just stay here and look at the fog, either – if we do, our situation hems us in and things start to feel more and more impossible.

So we go back to checking the obvious solutions. *Have I checked this column, and this row? Are there any obvious answers when I focus on this particular area?*

In the harder levels of Sudoku, we learned to look past the obvious and practice seeing what isn't there, as my daughter calls it. *If a green is already in this row but not in this 3x3 square, it must show up somewhere else in that square...but not in any of the columns it already appears in.*

In the fog and the wandering – or, the wondering – we combine the foundational principles with hard thinking, and for me this means journaling. It is another way to abide, to get thoughts down on paper where we can see what we're really dealing with. Then we can hold them up to Him to see if they line up with truth.

> *As long as our attention is turned upon ourselves and our own experiences...it is turned away from the Lord. This is plain common sense. As I have said elsewhere, we can only see the thing we look at, and while we are looking at ourselves, we simply cannot "behold God." It is not that He hides Himself; He is always there in full view of all who look unto Him; but if we are looking in another direction, we cannot expect to see Him.*
> – Hannah Whitall Smith 7

In that season of aimlessness I happened to be starting a new journal, which always feels momentous – the first or last page seems a little like a birthday or New Year's Day, as though it should summarize what's behind or set precedent for what's ahead. Of course, it doesn't really; that's a lot of pressure to put on one page of writing.

But those pages still feel weightier than all the pages between, and trying to decide what to write on them often reminds me of those sixth-grade journaling assignments when we had to write a certain number of words first thing in the morning. Our teacher would've already written a random subject on the board and we just needed to rattle on about it for two hundred words or so.

(Once, the subject was "cake," which I thought was extremely stupid – cake being a boring subject to me because I've always been more of a pie person. This, of course, was before I experienced the wonder known as tiramisu. Turns out, even cake can be made interesting if enough coffee, rum, and mascarpone are involved.)

I hated those assignments, but like many things, I look back and see the value in it – it was like finger exercises for my future, and I can only imagine how that teacher would gloat if she knew that journaling is something I assign myself now. It's not just part of my work; it holds me accountable to process and articulate things that would otherwise just simmer and evaporate, leaving mysterious sediment behind instead of resolution and answers.

For those who live according to the flesh set their minds on the things of the flesh, but those who live according to the Spirit set their minds on the things of the Spirit. For to set the mind on the flesh is death, but to set the mind on the Spirit is life and peace.
- Romans 8:5-6

So I wrote in that new journal, spilling words out about relationships and events and decisions to be made, about pain we were dealing with and things we hoped for, and about our need to hear from God so we could make the right moves with certainty:

The wind is shaking the windows here. It's dark out already – probably has been dark for an hour or so – and it'll be quiet for a few minutes until the next gust comes, rattling the panes and throwing debris against the window.

And though it's not the topic I'd choose to start a new journal with (just as I hate starting it with such awful handwriting), it can't be helped – the storm and the wind reflect our situation in such a perfect parallel, and we feel all the threats and gusts attempting to shake us in the darkness, and some days our faith feels like a thin wall that barely keeps us from rattling, or blowing over, or blowing away.

So I wish this first page of messy scrawling was more...successful. Victorious. And maybe it is, maybe the real success and victory are won in the muddy trenches when we still feel overrun by the enemy but we've refused to give up fighting, believing that reinforcements are still on the way.

We win the battle when we are tempted to resent but we choose instead to bless and forgive, when we're tempted to despair but choose to hope, or when we're tempted to complain and choose to rejoice. **We win by seeing what isn't there.** And the only way to see those things is to keep our eyes on Him.

He will show us how and when to move with certainty, regardless of the fog and questions around us. Reinforcements are still on the way.

be Thou my vision

DALLAN FORGAILL, 6TH CENTURY
TRANSLATED FROM OLD IRISH

Be Thou my vision, O lord of my heart;
Nought be all else to me, save that Thou art;
Thou my best thought, in the day and the night,
Waking or sleeping, Thy presence my light.

Be Thou my wisdom, be Thou my true word;
I ever with Thee, and Thou with me Lord;
Thou my Great Father, and I Thy true son;
Thou in me dwelling and I with Thee one.

Be Thou my breast-plate, my sword for the fight;
Be Thou my armour, and be Thou my might.
Thou my soul's shelter, and Thou my high tower:
Raise Thou me Heavenward, O power of my power.

Riches I heed not, nor man's empty praise,
Thou mine inheritance, through all my days:
Thou and Thou only, the first in my heart,
High King of Heaven, my treasure Thou art.

High King of Heaven when the battle is done,
Grant Heaven's joy to me, bright heaven's sun!
Christ of my own heart, whatever befall,
Still be thou my vision, O Ruler of all.

bedrock:
when nothing is working

In moments of desperate need, I can't tell you how many times I've heard this statement:

"God is never late, but He's rarely early."

And it sounds true – but is it, really? Is it a self-fulfilling prophecy? Or is it Biblical? Or is it generally false, but we're not paying enough attention to all the times God answers us ahead of time?

We talked it through, He and I. And here's what I learned about myself:

I have often feared that God would deliver the answers or breakthrough I needed at the very last moment possible *because I had to prove my steadfast faith in the meantime.* This would somehow show Him how much I deserved the answer I wanted. And when we untangled it and I saw it in that light, God revealed that this tendency had nothing to do with my trust in Him, and everything to do with me still thinking I could earn grace.

Many of us feel like we need to sweat it out for a while to show God we're worthy of breakthrough – as though we have to earn it by our stress level.

And sure, sometimes He is just in time. Sometimes we have to wait a long time for the answer, and sometimes the answer still isn't what we wanted.

But more often than not, God is early, showing up before we need Him to. We have food in our fridge and running water and clothes in our closets because He showed up early, instead of dropping food off at our doorstep when we're down to the last crumb. We drive in all weathers and almost always make it safe and drama-free to our destinations. We have normal, boring trips to the grocery store or post office, and nothing tragic happens.

What if we only recognize those last-minute, edge-of-our-seats, by-the-seat-of-our-pants victories because we are so blinded to His early and overflowing provision that we don't even recognize it?

Or do we take credit for those provisions, as though we did them on our own without His help?

God is early most of the time. It just happens so often that we take His early timing for granted.

Maybe we expect the last-minute breakthrough because those are the dramatic ones that we most remember. Or sometimes we experience a last minute-breakthrough because it matches our expectations, resulting in a circular self-fulfilling prophecy...because we prayed according to our expectations and not according to His greatness, and we got what we asked for.

But just because that's how it happens sometimes doesn't mean it's the standard precept. **Expecting God to come at the last minute is not the Biblical standard we should hope for.**

What if we started praying now like we usually pray at the last minute? What if we believed breakthrough and answers were imminent, and on the way? We've been longing for some things for years. What if we were brave enough to start praying with expectation again?

A friend once sent me this quote in a letter: *Don't try to get them to drop the silver. Just keep reaching out to them with the gold and they will drop the silver and reach for the gold themselves.*

And it resonated as truth with me, but we had a child with special needs that seemed to prove it wrong. Nothing seemed to work – we saw no cooperation, no effort, and no accomplishment, and we wondered when he would finally reach for the gold we offered. He seemed to think the gold was poison. We had no idea how long it would take to convince him that the gold meant healing, joy, freedom, and progress, and that those things weren't a threat to him and his security.

> *Although I can't say that I liked school, when I wanted to be I was a good enough student....I was, they said, like a good horse who would not work; I was a disappointment to them; I was wasting my God-given talents. And this gave me, I believe, the only self-determining power I had: I could withhold this single thing that was mine that I knew they wanted.*
> - Wendell Berry 8

And, man...we wanted progress for him. And he knew we wanted it.

But the further we went, the more we realized that early childhood trauma wired this child's belief system into a deep pit of lies, and there was no easy answer to luring him to drop the silver. He clung to it for dear life. He had fashioned it into a silver shovel engraved all over with words like control, fear, anxiety, grief, anger, and denial, and he used that thing to dig a deeper hole for himself almost daily.

But inside that hole, God had provided a golden staircase that went all the way down, to infinity and beyond, and the path to freedom was always there for the choosing. Our son acted like he was on a mission to see how deep the hole could get, to see if the golden staircase really extended as far as he could go.

They've known rejection and abandonment, and they test with every broken tool they've gathered to see if we will reject and abandon them, too.

"Will you really care for me? Even when I push you away? Even if I repulse you, are you really for real? If I persist in self-destruct mode, will you really stay, for good, forever?"

- from Upside Down: Understanding and Supporting Attachment in Adoptive and Foster Families [9]

And years later, that golden staircase *was* still there – but as the mom who watched him continue to test its depth, I wondered if there would come a point when it got so dark he couldn't even see it. Or, if he went that far, would the staircase still seem like a golden offer? Or would the effort to climb back out seem like too much work?

How long do we watch someone dig their own grave? How long do we wait for answers and breakthrough?

And, how do we pray for breakthrough when we expect God to not show up until the last minute?

How many fears must we face until then? How much trial do we expect to go through before we think He'll finally show up? That is daunting and terrifying to think about.

We can't make our kids make the right choices, but we can be brave and keep hoping and trying and offering. I'll be honest; I'm not always that brave. Many days I dread the attempt to offer gold, remembering how many times it's been rejected.

Sometimes being brave means letting ourselves feel all the feelings, like frustration and inadequacy and futility. It means facing the fears head-on, knowing that we can't earn the outcome we want when someone else's choices determine that outcome – but we can trust that God is good and has good for us regardless of whatever that particular outcome is.

> *Likewise the Spirit helps us in our weakness. For we do not know what to pray for as we ought, but the Spirit himself intercedes for us with groanings too deep for words. And he who searches hearts knows what is the mind of the Spirit, because the Spirit intercedes for the saints according to the will of God. And we know that for those who love God all things work together for good, for those who are called according to his purpose.*
>
> *- Romans 8:26-28*

Sometimes bravery looks like asking God for a new strategy, because we, too, have to be willing to drop the silver for gold.

My silver is the predictability of the status quo. Which, compared to my son's silver shovel of control, is kind of the same thing.

What we expect and ask for is often what we get. So, what if we had greater expectations? What if we prayed differently, and didn't wait until the last minute to expect Him to come through?

What if we expected breakthrough any time now?

> *For we know that the whole creation has been groaning together in the pains of childbirth until now. And not only the creation, but we ourselves, who have the firstfruits of the Spirit, groan inwardly as we wait eagerly for adoption as sons, the redemption of our bodies. For in this hope we were saved. Now hope that is seen is not hope. For who hopes for what he sees? But if we hope for what we do not see, we wait for it with patience.*
>
> *- Romans 8:22-25*

I didn't even know what to ask for, so I asked God how to pray for our son.

He said, *Ask Me to make him hit bedrock.*

And then ask Me to start filling the hole with water. If he refuses to swim, I will drive him to the staircase. Either way, he will rise up.

So that's what we asked, and are often still asking, and I don't know exactly what it will look like in the long run. But I think it will look something like turning his hole into a lake, and filling it – he will rest in the Living Water, and surrender control to the One who knows how to wield it.

I think it will look like God taking an issue that drains the life out of us, and making us all feel alive again. And I think He'll do it sooner than we would normally dare to hope for. Because more often than not, He shows up sooner than we expect.

at His word
BY RENEE PETTY

And Pilate again said to them, "Then what shall I do with the man you call the King of the Jews?"

And they cried out again, "Crucify him."

And Pilate said to them, "Why? What evil has he done?"

But they shouted all the more, "Crucify him!"

- Mark 15:12-14

Crucify him. The question I often ask myself when I read the accounts of Jesus' crucifixion is, "How?" How in the world did they not only miss the truth that Jesus was the long-awaited Messiah, but they also wanted Him dead, crucified, humiliated, crushed? What happened between the time the prophecies about Jesus were given and His arrival on the scene to transform their hearts from hope to hatred?

The answer is simple, yet not so – and completely wrapped up in our human nature. Hundreds of years passed between the first prophecies foretelling the coming of the Messiah and the time Jesus was born in Bethlehem. Years of waiting and hoping, of difficulty and Roman oppression, generations passing to the next. So much time to consider, to dissect, to attempt to figure out what God meant when He spoke of the Messiah. During that time many began to paint a picture of what Jesus would be, what He would do, when He came at last to His people.

They became *so fixated on their ideal of Jesus*, they missed the real thing. Jesus was common, He did not overthrow Rome, He chastised the religious leaders, He served the lowly, spoke the Truth with authority and did not obey the social mores of the day. He was nothing they wanted, and they hated Him for it. They did not understand His purpose, and in the end, their hatred was used by Him to fulfill the very promise they failed to grasp.

How often have I been guilty of failing to take God at His word in seasons of waiting? How many times have I, too, filled in the blanks with my own ideas, desires, and dreams? Have I missed seeing

the promise because I no longer recognized it? And yet, the amazing thing about God is He will do what He says He will do, period.

In hope [Abraham] believed against hope, *that he should become the father of many nations, as he had been told, "So shall your offspring be." He did not weaken in faith when he considered his own body, which was as good as dead (since he was about a hundred years old), or when he considered the barrenness of Sarah's womb. No unbelief made him waver concerning the promise of God, but he grew strong in his faith as he gave glory to God,* **fully convinced that God was able to do what he had promised.**

- Romans 4:18-21

Paul, the writer of Romans, remembers Abraham as a man of great faith, and yet we know that Abraham got anxious while waiting and tried to make it happen on his own by having a son with Sarah's servant. What is the difference between Abraham and those who cried for the crucifixion of Jesus? When Abraham lost sight of the promise, he always came back to the words God had spoken to him. He was willing to surrender *his dream* to God, even surrender his son, because he trusted that God, who spoke, would deliver.

What promise are you waiting for, friend? What has God spoken to you about that feels so far from fulfilled? Do not give in to the temptation to figure out the how and when. Do not determine what that promise will look like exactly or try to make it happen in your timing. Ephesians 3:20 says, *Now to him who is able to do far more abundantly than all that we ask or think, according to the power at work within us.* **Abundantly more**, more than you can think, more than you can ask – which means you're probably going to get it all wrong anyway. Instead, take Him at His word. Trust in Him, press into Him, do not lose hope, and be *fully convinced* that the God who promised will be faithful to you.

doing the work

Oh, peonies, those big flirts. By late afternoon on the same day I pick them, they're already fading.

They're just like the excitement of new projects – the idea and inspiration phase, when we dream big. We imagine gigantic peonies, and think of how gorgeous they will be in bloom.

But then we start thinking of the discipline it takes to follow through with those dreams and actually do the work. And the work is harder, riskier, uncharted territory. We know that peonies wilt quickly. We wonder if it's worth the effort to start, or to push through.

> *All hard work brings a profit,*
> * but mere talk leads only to poverty.*
> - Proverbs 14:23

And sometimes we give up right there. Nope, those big dreams, those giant peonies – someone else can have them, we tell ourselves. We'll just let dandelions grow there instead. But it leaves us empty. And when we shrink back and give up, we are the ones who wilt.

So, pardon me while I break out the loudspeaker for Exodus 35:

> *Let every skillful craftsman among you come and make all that the Lord has commanded.*
> - Exodus 35:10

Friend, in case you need a boost, a nudge, or a friendly kick in the pants...He's still telling this to His people.

Sometimes when we read the Bible we get lost in these sticky pages, chapter after chapter of detail on laws, genealogy, battles, or whatever. The repetition and minute description is our clue that this stuff is important to God.

Accuracy is important. History is important. Good conduct is important.

All the work is important.

A good part of Exodus is chapter after chapter of details about the tabernacle: textiles, woodwork, carpentry, engraving, on and on. Because creativity, art, and craftsmanship are important to God, too.

God created, and He made that creation to grow, flourish, and reproduce. To be prolific, even when battered and torn.

And we are the Created, too – participating in the creative process, growing deep and wide, healing, renewing, learning, (re)producing, always meant for more.

> *From the fruit of their lips people are filled with good things,*
>   *and the work of their hands brings them reward.*
> - Proverbs 12:14

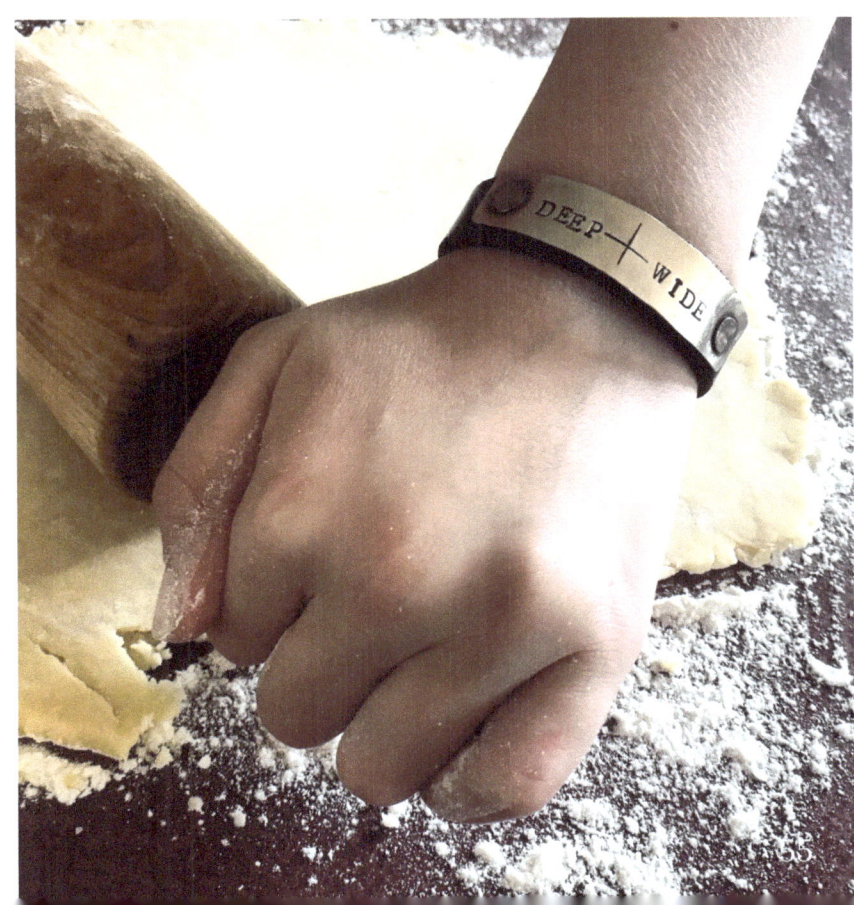

You know what? Those peonies *do* wilt quickly. And those dreams will make you work harder than you ever thought you could. But you know what else?

You'll have a stronger root system. The foundation you grow from will reach deeper and wider than it did before. And next year, you'll have more peonies than you ever had before. You might share them with friends, or venture into growing something else, too.

So go do that amazing thing you do. Do not neglect the gifting He's given you. When you see how the world needs it, you won't be sorry you did the work.

favorite salad
& croutons

This salad is light and sweet and perfect for crowds and gatherings, or to keep for yourself so you have easy lunches ready for the week. If you can make salad addicting, that's a good thing.

The croutons are optional but the vinaigrette isn't – and it is, well, more like a *pineapplegrette* anyway. Like most throw-together recipes, I saw a version of this in a book years ago and have modified it to the point of unrecognizability, changing ingredients and adding croutons and completely reworking the dressing. So this recipe is now mine, but given to you, to modify accordingly again. Measurements are approximate; go according to your own taste and preferences.

Ingredients for salad:
1 head of lettuce (I prefer red leaf)
½ onion, thinly sliced
½ apple or pear, thinly sliced
¼ cup raisins or dried cranberries
¼ cup finely chopped pineapple
¼ cup chopped pecans or walnuts
A handful of pumpkin seeds or sunflower seeds
1 t. butter or olive oil
A little feta, if you like

Ingredients for viniagrette:
¼ cup pineapple juice
2 T. apple cider vinegar...or kombucha
2. T. olive oil
¼ t. cinnamon
¼ t. ginger
A shake of black pepper and salt

1 Melt the butter or oil in a small saucepan and sauté the onions on low until they are translucent and golden.

2 While the onions are sautéing, chop the lettuce and combine it in a big bowl with all the remaining salad ingredients except the feta.

3 Check your onions. As soon as they're cooked, remove from heat and allow to cool.

4 Make dressing: Add all vinaigrette ingredients to a jar, close tightly, and shake like crazy.

5 Add the cooled onions to the salad. Drizzle half the dressing over the salad. Toss salad, then drizzle the rest.

6 Have croutons and feta handy on the side so they don't get soggy from the dressing.

croutons

Ingredients:
2 or 3 slices of a sweet bread of your choice (shown is cinnamon raisin)
1-2 t. olive oil or butter

1 Slice the bread into cubes.

2 Add olive oil/butter to small saucepan and turn heat to medium low.

3 Add the bread cubes and gently stir to coat with the butter or oil. Allow to brown for a couple of minutes, stir, and brown some more.

4 Add to your salad – or feed to your toddler, if he finds them first.

vegan gluten-free banana bread

BY MĒGAN ANCHETA

makes 1 loaf

When my oldest daughter went through a period of needing to avoid eggs, this was the banana bread recipe I created for her. It's a very popular recipe with my family and blog readers! Regular or non-organic sugars will work just fine in this recipe.

ingredients:
4 medium-sized ripe bananas, peeled and mashed
1/2 cup organic brown sugar
1/4 cup organic cane sugar
6 tablespoons coconut oil, melted (or vegan butter)
6 tablespoons water
1 teaspoon vanilla extract, optional
3/4 cup sorghum flour
1/2 cup brown rice flour
1/2 cup tapioca starch
1 1/2 teaspoons baking soda
1 teaspoon xanthan gum
1 teaspoon ground cinnamon
1/2 teaspoon ground nutmeg
1/2 teaspoon sea salt
3/4 cup dairy-free chocolate chips

1. Preheat oven to 350 degrees (F). Line a 9"x5" bread pan with parchment paper and generously grease.

2. In a large bowl, mix together the mashed banana, organic brown sugar, and organic cane sugar, melted coconut oil, water, and vanilla extract.

3. In a separate mixing bowl, whisk together the sorghum flour, brown rice flour, tapioca starch, baking soda, xanthan gum, ground cinnamon, ground nutmeg, and sea salt.

4. Pour the dry ingredients into the wet and mix until just blended.

5. Stir in the dairy-free chocolate chips.

6. Pour the batter into the prepared bread pan, and bake for 50-55 minutes, or until a toothpick, when inserted into the center of the loaf, comes out mostly clean.

7. Allow the loaf to cool for 10 minutes in the pan before removing and placing on a wire rack. Cool completely before slicing.

the fruit we bear

I have no idea what kind of citrus plants these are; our daughter planted them years ago from a jar of old mixed seeds. They came up quickly but then seemed to stagnate; they were healthy, just super slow about growing bigger in spite of fertilizer, repotting, and the best light in the house we could give them.

Some areas in our lives are just like that. They start off with enthusiasm, but then sort of fall off and seem to hang in limbo. The leaves are lush but not increasing. And we don't know if they'll ever bear fruit anyway, or even what that fruit will be.

Are we growing oranges, God, or grapefruit? Or something else entirely? Or are we just wasting time in hibernation?

And when I struggle with this (and oh, have I struggled with this!) He reminds me that His kingdom is of increase. Not every seed we plant bears fruit, sure – but those that do produce more seeds in the hundreds and thousands.

He is not wasting our time as we plant and tend and watch, waiting for clarity and direction.

God wants us to hear Him. He's not messing around, and He doesn't play tricks on us about this. So often we think we struggle with hearing God, but what we really struggle with is believing His goodness.

> *In him we have redemption through his blood, the forgiveness of our trespasses, according to the riches of his grace, which he lavished upon us,* **in all wisdom and insight making known to us the mystery of his will, according to his purpose***, which he set forth in Christ as a plan for the fullness of time, to unite all things in him, things in heaven and things on earth.*
> *– Ephesians 1:7-10*

What we really struggle with is trusting Him, because we've been around and we've seen how this stuff can go down, and we're not always used to being treated like a loved one by those we love.

But we're His beloved. And His ways are not our ways[10] (we can recite this all day long, but do we believe it?) and His character and ways are not diminished or demeaned by our experience or expectations.

He speaks. We hear Him when we listen. And listening means, well, *listening*, but also reading His word and asking Him for clarity – which He is eager to give. It means asking questions, and He is eager to answer. It means talking to His people and hearing confirmation and truth through an experienced friend. And sometimes it means waiting for a new direction, because He is a good Father who knows what we need and when we need it.

But it never means just waiting for the next shoe to drop. It never means He's teasing or testing you to see if you're paying attention. It never means He's being evasive. It never means He's annoyed with you.

His ways are not our ways; He's a better parent than we are. And He always wants to talk to – and hear – His kids.

The thing to ask ourselves when we're unsettled is this: Am I doing what He already told me to? Or am I avoiding that and trying to distract myself with this other frantic movement, spinning my wheels?

Am I really supposed to be doing something different? (Maybe.) Or am I just having a hard time trusting Him and waiting? (Also maybe.)

He has not dropped the ball. He hasn't disregarded you, ignored you, or blown you off. He is actively moving on our behalf and for our good in ways that are often far too complex for us to understand. If we hold still and wait when He tells us to, we'll be out of the way so His work can be accomplished, and at the same time we'll be in the right place to cooperate with that work when we're called to do so. We won't miss the call when we're listening to receive it, being faithful in the things He already gave us to do. God is faithful to cultivate the dreams He puts in us when we trust Him, obeying in bold, risky ways.

We are faithful to water, to watch, and to pray, and He is faithful to use the process to grow and increase...us. Because we are the ones He is growing, and He doesn't waste a thing.

This is the season we spent digging deep and wide for, preparing for the victories and breakthrough we've been transitioning toward.

We've been through the waiting. And while we were waiting, He was waiting for us to be okay with waiting, for us to be settled in Him regardless of how unsettled anything else was. He was waiting for our hearts to be in fermata, at rest, quiet and confident and expectant and unshaken.

The last season was the scaffold we are building the next season on. And the days ahead are good. He hasn't wasted a moment of our grief and effort and seeking – yours and mine. All of those seeds we thought were dead and buried were just waiting for the right season to shoot out, sprouting new life: vibrant, fruit-bearing, deep and wide, both in our underground roots and in our branches skyward. We will be the ones leafing out, carrying shade and shelter.

...we have not ceased to pray for you,
asking that you may be filled
with the knowledge of his will
in all spiritual *wisdom* and *understanding*,
so as to walk in a manner worthy of the Lord,
fully pleasing to him:
bearing fruit in every good work
and increasing in the *knowledge* of God.

– colossians 1:9-10

study guide

This flexible, light-yoked guide is for you to use on your own or with a small group. We've included questions to use for personal journaling or group discussion, scripture to study, copy down, and memorize, and short prompts for prayer. It's not homework or another thing to add to your list – it's just movement forward and rest for your soul, friends.

toward victory

questions

What situation am I most longing to see progress in, currently?

How can I pray in a new way toward that progress?

What can I say to God right now about it?

scripture

Psalm 31:19, 1 Thessalonians 4:11

prayer

God, thank You for using my faithfulness to show me Your faithfulness. Help me to steadily continue in obedience and keep my eyes toward victory.

one stitch at a time

questions

How has God made my identity secure in Him?

What limits has He placed on me? What limits have I imposed on myself that I might need to reconsider?

How is the structure of those limits directing my movement in this season?

scripture

Ephesians 1:3-6

prayer

Lord, You know exactly where I'm headed and when I am going to get there. You know what is coming after that and You know how to prepare me for the next level. Please give me Your vision of where I'm headed, and help me to see this season with your perspective.

He makes us to see

questions

How can I recognize God's voice speaking to me?

How can I better prepare myself to recognize when other voices vie for my attention?

What will I do when I first realize I am listening to the wrong voice, and how will I refocus on God?

scripture

2 Timothy 3:16-17, John 8:47, John 10:27-28, Psalm 25:4-5

prayer

Father, Thank You that You want me to hear Your voice. Please help me to recognize You speaking to me and help me to listen to You alone. Help me to recognize wrong voices immediately and to take those thoughts captive, giving them to You to be replaced with truth.

sounding it out

questions

What am I struggling with that seems like it might have a really simple solution?

In what current situation am I obeying without seeing? How is God leading me in it?

Where do I see my desires coming into alignment with God's desires for me?

scripture

Hebrews 11:1-8, 1 John 4:18

prayer

Holy Spirit, help me to be so attuned to Your direction that I do not doubt it when I hear it. Thank You for knowing my heart and bringing me into alignment with Your heart.

a surrendered focus

questions

What longings do I have that I know God wants to fulfill?

What longings do I have that are less certain? Why am I unsure about them?

What does surrendering my focus look like right now?

scripture

1 John 3:1-3, 18-24

prayer

Dear Jesus, I surrender these longings to You and ask You to show me how You feel about them. Thank You for helping me to see the way You do, and give me wisdom to pursue these longings in the best ways.

out of the comfort zone, into the mess

questions

Do I tend to recognize my weakness, or pretend expertise?

Where is God calling me to step out of the comfort zone in order to step toward a dream?

What does obeying in that look like?

scripture

Habakkuk 2:2-4

prayer

God, thank You for preparing me for the callings You've put on my life. Thank You for using me now and for growing me as I walk into this new season. Give me Your words as I write the vision, so I can match it to Your will.

murky waters

questions

What is one clear area that the Lord is highlighting to me in this season?

What is He dreaming of in this situation? What is He seeing that I can't?

What has the Lord done in the past for me or others to build our faith when things are murky?

scripture

Isaiah 33:2, 1 Thessalonians 3:6-13

prayer

God, I will trust You when things happen that I did not expect. You are not surprised when I am and you are not dismayed when I don't understand the timing of events. Please help me to be at peace as I walk in patience.

seeing what isn't there

questions

Where have I been wandering and restless?

Looking back, how has God prepared me for this time in my life?

Where do I need to bless and forgive instead of resent? What am I tempted to complain about that I can flip to rejoicing, instead?

scripture

Romans 8:5-11

prayer

Thank You, Father, for walking with me even when I did not recognize You or understand what You were doing. My eyes are on You, and You are bringing all the help and answers I need.

bedrock

questions

Where in my life has God been consistently early, and I've just taken it for granted?

For what situation do I need to start bravely praying with expectation?

What am I avoiding praying about because I don't want to feel all the feelings? How can I move forward in that as I pray right now?

scripture

Romans 8:22-28

prayer

Holy Spirit, please give me new strategy in this situation. Help me to walk in bold, brave obedience, trusting You with my heart.

at His word

questions

Have I been so fixated on my ideal that I've missed God's answer for a situation?

Where have I been tempted to fill in the blanks with my own ideas, desires, and dreams?

What does his promise look like when I move my preconceived ideas out of the way?

scripture

Mark 15:12-14, Romans 4:18-21, Ephesians 3:20

prayer

Jesus, You never break a promise and You are true to Your word. You will deliver above and beyond all I can imagine, even when circumstances catch me off guard.

doing the work

questions

What has God made me a "skillful craftsman" in? How can I develop a stronger root system in that?

How might the world benefit from me using that gifting?

scripture

Exodus 35:4-35

prayer

God, thank You for giving me skills to develop and grow in. Help me to lean in to the work You're calling me to, and have discernment to know what You're not calling me to.

the fruit we bear

questions

Where have I planted in faith, not knowing exactly what the result would be?

Am I doing what He already told me to? Or am I avoiding that and trying to distract myself with this other frantic movement, spinning my wheels?

How has God been growing me as I watch and wait and pray?

scripture

Ephesians 1:7-10

prayer

Holy Spirit, You are bringing new life in the perfect season. Thank You for using my efforts, and bearing fruit through me.

notes

1. Charlotte Mason, *Ourselves* (Quarryville, Penn: Charlotte Mason Research and Supply, 1989), 188.

2. *"For who has understood the mind of the Lord so as to instruct him?" But we have the mind of Christ.* – 1 Corinthians 2:16

3. *There is no fear in love, but perfect love casts out fear. For fear has to do with punishment, and whoever fears has not been perfected in love.* – 1 John 4:18

4. George MacDonald, *Lilith* (Holicong, PA: Wildside Press, no date given), 261.

5. "Proverbs 3: King James Version," Blue Letter Bible, www.blueletterbible.org/kjv/pro/3/1/t_conc_631005.

6. *But I am not ashamed, for I know whom I have believed, and I am convinced that he is able to guard until that day what has been entrusted to me.* – 2 Timothy 1:12b

7. Hannah Whitall Smith, *The God of All Comfort* (Westwood, NJ: The Christian Library, 1984), 199-200.

8. Wendell Berry, *Jayber Crow* (Berkeley, CA: Counterpoint Press, 2000), 33-34.

9. Shannon Guerra, *Upside Down: Understanding and Supporting Attachment in Adoptive and Foster Families* (Wasilla, Alaska: Copperlight Wood, 2019), 8.

10. *For my thoughts are not your thoughts, neither are your ways my ways, declares the LORD.* – Isaiah 55:8

also by shannon guerra

the Work That God Sees series
prayerful motherhood in the midst of the overwhelm

Moms, you pour yourselves out every day. How about some powerful refilling, in small, easy doses?

Short chapters. White space. Deep down hope, and out loud laughter. Because you have what it takes. You are watched over and known by the God who notices every detail, and He meets you in these mundane moments and is breathing them into mighty movement.

Work That God Sees is available as six individual little books, or as a complete, all-in-one edition with the content from all six books (including the snarky recipes, crafty patterns, and questions for personal journaling or small group discussion) plus 25 pages of extra stories, recipes, and lessons you can learn at someone else's expense.

Oh My Soul

encountering God in honest, unconventional (and sometimes messy) prayer

What if there was **one thing** you could do that would always, without fail, make you more **whole** and **healed** and **at peace** than you were the day before…would you do it?

What if, at the same time, that one thing transformed the world around you?

This is what happens when we encounter God, living in His presence, in continual conversation with Him.

We want to hear God better, and to know His will for all the messy, mundane details of our life. But does He still speak to us when we are distracted, grumpy, overwhelmed, and unprepared? How can we have "quiet time" with God when there's no quiet, and no time? Can we really know the will of God and move forward in obedience, in spite of our fears and failures?

And, if we're really honest with Him, will He strike us with lightning? Or will we end up praying with boldness and authenticity like never before?

Available as the original book, companion journal, and 21-day devotional study.

upside down

understanding and supporting attachment in adoptive and foster families

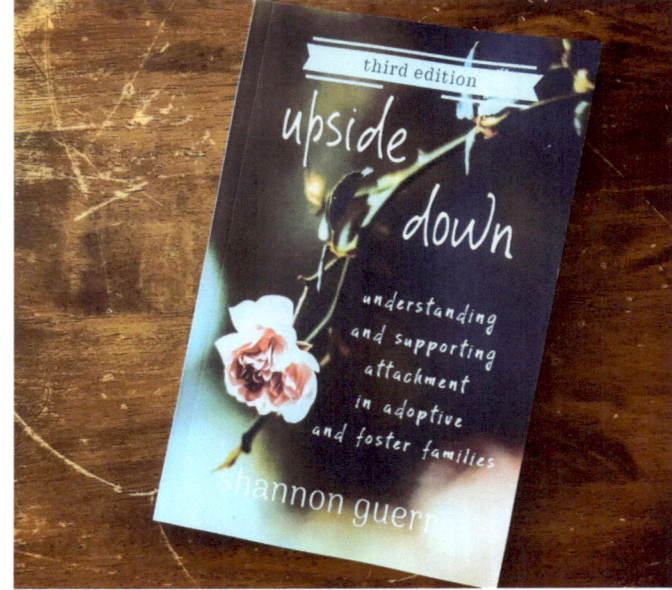

This book gives hope to adoptive and foster families, and the lowdown for those who love them.

Adoptive and foster families working through attachment issues often feel alone, but their communities can intentionally be part of the solution instead of unintentionally being part of the problem. Without that support, adoptive and foster families live in isolation.

Shannon Guerra learned this firsthand after she and her husband adopted two of their children in 2012. She started writing shockingly transparent blog posts about what her family was going through at home, at the doctor's office, and in her heart as a mama.

And then adoptive and foster families started writing back.

Their overwhelming, unanimous theme was, **"This is what I've wanted to tell people for so long. I wish everyone who knows our family could read this."**

This book is the result. In about 100 pages, *Upside Down* provides information and insight that transforms an outsider's assumptions into an insider's powerful perspective. Because adoptive and foster families should never feel alone, and our communities can be equipped to make sure they never feel that way again.

the ABIDE series
a year of growing deep + wide

volume titles:

rest in the running

hope in the waiting

clarity in the longing

bravery for the next step

obedience to move forward

surrendering to win

ABIDE is off the beaten path: A 6-volume series of fully illustrated books that are part devotional, part coffee table book, part magazine. These six beautiful books will lead you further into the presence of God as you grow deep and wide, pressing forward in these seasons that stretch us. Each book contains full color photographs, a light-yoked study section for personal or small group use, an extra recipe or two, and powerful encouragement that meets you where you're at and moves you forward.

one more thing...

Need a little white space in the chaos?

You are warmly invited to copperlightwood.com, where we're transparent about finding peace in the hard moments and beauty in the mess. I hope you'll hit the subscribe button and poke around all the posts and videos. Just keep in mind that it's a little unpolished here, so watch out for the Legos on the floor.

Bless you, friend,
Shannon Guerra

connect:
parler: shannonguerra
mewe: shannonguerra
gab: shannonguerra
clouthub: shannonguerra
facebook: copperlightwood
instagram: copperlightwood
goodreads: shannonguerra
pinterest: copperlightwood

email:
shannon@copperlightwood.com